Hosea

DISCOVER TOGETHER BIBLE STUDY SERIES

Leader's guides are available at www.discovertogetherseries.com

A *Discover Together*
BIBLE STUDY

Hosea

Discovering God's Fierce Love

Sue Edwards

Kregel
Publications

ISBN 978-0-8254-4439-5

Printed in the United States of America
19 20 21 22 23 24 25 26 27 28 / 5 4 3 2 1

Contents

How to Get the Most Out of a Discover Together Bible Study

Women today need Bible study to keep balanced, focused, and Christ-centered in their busy worlds. The tiered questions in *Hosea: Discovering God's Fierce Love* allow you to choose a depth of study that fits your lifestyle, which may even vary from week to week, depending on your schedule.

Just completing the basic questions will require about one and a half hours per lesson and will provide a basic overview of the text. For busy women, this level offers in-depth Bible study with a minimum time commitment.

"Digging Deeper" questions are for those who want to, and make time to, probe the text even more deeply. Answering these questions may require outside resources such as an atlas, Bible dictionary, or concordance; you may be asked to look up parallel passages for additional insight; or you may be encouraged to investigate the passage using an interlinear Greek-English text or *Vine's Expository Dictionary*. This deeper study will challenge you to learn more about the history, culture, and geography related to the Bible, and to grapple with complex theological issues and differing views. Some with teaching gifts and an interest in advanced academics will enjoy exploring the depths of a passage and might even find themselves creating outlines and charts and writing essays worthy of seminarians!

This inductive Bible study is designed for both individual and group discovery. You will benefit most if you tackle each week's lesson on your own and then meet with other women to share insights, struggles, and aha moments. Bible study leaders will find a free, downloadable leader's guide for each study, along with general tips for leading small groups, at www.discovertogetherseries.com.

Choose a realistic level of Bible study that fits your schedule. You may want to finish the basic questions first and then "dig deeper" as time permits. Take time to savor the questions, and don't rush through the application. Read the sidebars for additional insight to enrich the experience. Note the optional passage to memorize and determine if this discipline would be

helpful for you. Do not allow yourself to be intimidated by women who have more time or who are gifted differently.

Make your Bible study—whatever level you choose—top priority. Consider spacing your study throughout the week so that you can take time to ponder and meditate on what the Holy Spirit is teaching you. Do not make other appointments during the group Bible study. Ask God to enable you to attend faithfully. Come with an excitement to learn from others and a desire to share yourself and your journey. Give it your best, and remember that God promises to join you on this adventure that can change your life.

Why Study Hosea?

Have you ever plumbed the depths of Hosea to discover its beauty and practical wisdom for today? If not, you've missed a priceless treasure. Here's your opportunity to discover how much God really loves you, how much sin breaks his heart, and why his tough love is often his kindest act toward you and others.

Recently, I heard a woman say, "We need to stop teaching women that God loves them and instead teach them that God is holy." I understand her concern. Too many women see God as the great Santa Claus in the sky or someone to turn to when they need help out of a jam. But the Bible focuses on God's gracious love *and* his righteous holiness. We need a thorough understanding of both. Hosea intertwines these two great theological themes to give us an accurate picture of who God is and how he relates to us, even when we or others disappoint or betray him. He loves us with a fierce love, but a nonchalant, lackadaisical attitude toward him can result in unpleasant, sometimes painful, discipline. To understand these realities prepares us to navigate our circumstances with insight and to better understand God's work in the lives of others—all valuable lessons.

Hosea was one of twelve "minor" Old Testament prophets, labeled "minor" not because they were less important but because of the shorter length of their books. For hundreds of years, God had been sending prophets to warn the Israelites that betraying him could lead to serious consequences, but they closed their eyes and ears. So God implemented a teaching tool stronger than words, an object lesson. God asked Hosea to become an ongoing living metaphor, to use his own life to illustrate God's righteous, burning jealousy, fierce love, and redemptive discipline. He asked Hosea, the town preacher, to marry a prostitute named Gomer. "Go, marry a promiscuous woman and have children with her, for like an adulterous wife this land is guilty of unfaithfulness to the Lord" (Hosea 1:2).

In the marriage, Hosea represents God and Gomer represents the unfaithful Israelites. What would you do if God asked this of you? How would your hopes, dreams, and expectations change? Hosea obeyed, and his courage astounds me. I'm grateful he willingly and sacrificially took on

the role of God's object lesson to teach us profound truths that can help us live wisely today.

In his book, Hosea shares his life story and the sermons he preached to the wayward Israelites. In Hosea's writings, we observe a vacillating pattern as he moves from sections that express God's jealousy to sections that express the ultimate grace of God, and back again. He uses a variety of literary devices, prose, poetry, images, stories, and prophecies to challenge our minds, touch our hearts, and inspire us to reserve our highest devotion exclusively for God.

God's righteous jealousy is evident throughout the book—not the paranoia, distrust, unhealthy smothering, and possessiveness we observe in sick human relationships but God's courageous, redemptive love for his beloved's highest good. God chose the picture of a healthy marriage bond between one man and one woman to depict his relationship with us. How do you feel about God as your Lover/Husband? It's probably the most developed Old Testament imagery that God uses for our relationship with him. Also, Paul uses this imagery in Ephesians 5:29–32 when he calls the church the bride of Christ, and John speaks of the church as a bride in Revelation.

Scot McKnight wrote, "Prior to Hosea the relationship of God with Israel went something like this: 'I am your God' and 'you are my people.' After Hosea the relationship of God with Israel was 'I am your Lover and I want you, Israel, for myself.' Prior to Hosea no one dared to speak of God as a Lover" (*Jesus Creed*, 44).

As a woman, I find this imagery of God as Lover beautiful. I hope you will too. He created us with an innate desire to love and be loved, to know and be known so we could be in intimate relationship with him. He rightly expects this deep personal bond with us. Our thirst for perfect love won't be met here in this fallen world but only as ultimate fulfillment in a sweet union with the Lord in eternity—but we get a glimpse, a taste here, as Hosea brings these beautiful truths to life.

He lived during a time much like today. Many who had once loved God deeply were turning their backs on him to pursue idols promising fulfillment, love, and happiness only to find them empty, like Jude described in verse 12: "They are clouds without rain, blown along by the wind; autumn trees, without fruit and uprooted—twice dead." We live among similar idols hoping to lure us away from God at every corner. The Israelites refused to heed Hosea's warnings and endured a seventy-year captivity as a result. Hosea's book is included in God's Word to protect us from making the same mistake. Nevertheless, God brought the Israelites back into the promised land as a sign of his unconditional love for his own. In addition to protecting us, the book of Hosea should enable us to understand the relationship between God's righteous jealousy, his holiness, *and* his grace. What a gift!

Discovering God's Fierce Love

God teaches us about himself through creation. For example, we learn about God by looking at how he designed us. We experience personal love relationships, and since love is directed toward another person with hopes of reciprocity, we know that God is personal.

God designed us with intrinsic cravings to be loved. That need can be imperfectly met in this life through romantic affections and even *agape* forms of platonic and parental love. Romantic sentiments can blossom into marriages where we treat one another with fidelity, respect one another's dignity, and love one another well. When we experience that kind of healthy marriage, we can understand more fully God's tender affection for us.

But when either a husband or a wife betrays their spouse, the wounded partner often experiences deep, even devastating, hurt. We probably all remember a time when someone we cared for betrayed us. Was it in elementary school or high school or as an adult? Did you know that God also experiences this kind of deep heartache when his loved ones betray him? His response is righteous jealousy.

GOD PURSUES YOU WITH A FIERCE PASSION

God passionately desires intimacy with you right now. He insists that your relationship with him take top priority in your affections, above your love for all others, even covenant spouses, precious children, and special friends. Like a jealous lover, God will not share you with others—and the beauty of his ferocious love is pictured in the writings of the Old Testament prophet Hosea. He awakens us to the splendor of God's devotion and his demand that we reciprocate that devotion. He also shows us God's agony when our sin spoils this intimacy. Many of us have felt waves of that agony through the death of a loved one, the betrayal of vows, or the devastation of divorce.

God inspired Hosea to help us understand his jealous love for us through a true account—the story of Hosea's marriage to an unfaithful

OPTIONAL

Memorize
Romans 8:38–39
For I am convinced that neither death nor life, neither angels nor demons, neither the present nor the future, nor any powers, neither height nor depth, nor anything else in all creation, will be able to separate us from the love of God that is in Christ Jesus our Lord.

Have you ever considered why God created life with changing seasons? I believe they speak of the spiritual reality of redemption. Every year we experience the birth of life and growth in spring and summer, death in fall and winter, then new birth again in the spring, as the earth bursts into life after a cold, bare winter. —Sue

wife, Gomer, who betrayed him by going after other lovers. In this story, Hosea represents God and Gomer represents Israel, as well as all of us when we are unfaithful to God.

As you work your way through the book of Hosea, my hope and prayer are that you will discover the ferocious love of God for you in a brand-new way, and that this discovery will inflame you to devote yourself more fully to God as the supreme relationship in your life—now and forever.

OUR PERSONAL LONGING FOR LOVE

When I was a little girl, I was in love with love, as defined by the world. My daddy and I enjoyed tender playful times during my preschool and grade school days, but when I entered my teen years, he grew emotionally distant and preoccupied. An only child without the guidance of a Christian home, I sought to fill the hole in my heart through an obsession with romance. Starry-eyed, I'd flirt, find a boyfriend, and expect our relationship to mimic what I saw in the movies, and when it didn't, I'd look elsewhere. I wasn't promiscuous, but I loved to be cuddled and kissed, hoping that this encounter would meet the deep ache in my heart to be known and loved well. It never did. Later I married a good man and we found Christ together. We've spent more than four and a half decades together, going on five, and we love each other deeply. But even a healthy marriage hasn't totally filled that ache—and I've come to believe that it was never meant to. God created this desire within us to draw us to himself, now and for eternity. Digesting Hosea has strengthened that conviction even more.

THE UNIVERSAL LONGING FOR LOVE

Some in the media understand this ache and use it to their advantage. According to an article entitled "What Are the Most Popular Literary Genres?" romance fiction sells the best of any genre, generating $1.44 billion a year with a dedicated fan base of thirty million readers (Verrillo).

In her article "11 Romance Readers Reveal Why They Love the Genre," Stephanie Topacio Long describes why these books sell so well. One reader, Stephanie, 26, explained why she reads romance novels: "I've always loved reading the genre . . . because it satisfies the part of me that was never able to let go of childhood fairy tales." Molly, 29, added: "To me, romance novels are all about hope, hope for two people to find each other and fall madly in love and all will be OK. . . . Even though I know how they are going to end . . . I still like the hope/dream that a happily ever after is possible." Hear the universal ache to love and be loved well.

In addition, a recent media phenomenon illustrates this universal desire: Hallmark movies. Beginning in 2016, cable ratings for Hallmark movies jumped 28 percent, while everyone else's declined. Cristina Ford writes, "There's something at play here that goes beyond cheesy plots. . . . The predictable characters and déjà-vu story lines offer a stark contrast to our tumultuous world. They subconsciously give us a taste of the stability and comfort that we're so desperately seeking. That's why they work—and not just with your mom" ("Why Do Moms Prefer Hallmark Movies").

Whatever, your attitude toward romance novels, you must admit that they play on the reality that God created women with this personal and universal longing for love. How can our desire for connection find complete fulfillment? Journey with me through the pages of Hosea to find out.

HISTORICAL SETTING

Where does the prophet Hosea's ministry fit into biblical history? Here's a bird's-eye view:

- About 2000 BC, God founded the nation of Israel when he made a covenant with Abraham. His son Isaac had two sons, Jacob and Esau. Jacob became the father of twelve sons who became the twelve tribes of Israel.
- A famine relocated the twelve tribes to Egypt where they eventually were enslaved. After several hundred years, Moses led them to freedom and "the promised land" where they made their home and were ruled by various "judges."
- About 1000 BC, the Israelites demanded a king like the pagan nations around them had. God granted their desire by giving them a foolish king, Saul, and later David and his son Solomon.
- Under Solomon, Israel prospered, but because he did not follow the Lord, after his death the nation officially split in 931 BC. Ten tribes became the Northern Kingdom and they retained the name "Israel." The other two tribes living in the south became the Southern Kingdom and took on the name "Judah."

Hosea came on the scene during the time of the divided kingdom, and he spoke mostly to the Northern Kingdom, Israel, although his messages were appropriate for Judah, just as they are still fitting for us today. We'll discover the fate of both the Northern and Southern Kingdoms as we work our way through Hosea's six sermons.

Disclaimer: When Hosea penned his story and sermons into this book, God had made a conditional covenant with the nation Israel called the Mosaic covenant. If the nation loved and obeyed God, they would be blessed as a nation. If they did not, they would experience national curses. In our study we will observe the playing out of these national curses as consequences for their corporate sin. However, today, as church-age believers, we are not under the Mosaic covenant. We are under the unconditional new covenant in which God deals with each of us as individuals.

I used to hate [Hallmark movies] . . . for the same reasons I hated Thomas Kinkade paintings: . . . too tidy, too perfect, too idyllic—absent the pain, ugliness, and darkness that gives meaningful and resonant texture to real life. But then I noticed how much delight my in-laws got from watching these movies. . . . And then my wife and I started watching them too, not only to ridicule their ridiculousness (which we do), but also to find comfort in their beauty. Yes, their beauty.
—Brett McCracken ("Formulaic for a Reason")

Hosea through Malachi, the last twelve books in the Old Testament, are labeled "The Minor Prophets." These prophets warned the Israelites that God was grieving over their idolatry; he saw their disloyalty and lack of love for others and for him. Judgment would come in the form of exile to the lands of foreign conquerors, the Assyrians and Babylonians. They would suffer under these pagans' cruel treatment as a form of discipline to wake them up from their spiritual malaise. But the minor prophets also announced that after this discipline would come ultimate redemption and restoration, a beacon of hope calling them to purity, humility, justice, and love for God and others.   —Sue

Therefore, be careful in applying the predictions of national disaster we observe in Hosea to any nation today.

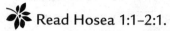 **Read Hosea 1:1–2:1.**

God asked Hosea to use his own love life to illustrate a spiritual reality that was occurring in Israel during those days and ever since.

1. What did God ask Hosea to do and why (1:2)? What would this mean for Hosea's life?

2. How would you feel if God asked you to do this? Why might you struggle to obey God if you were in this situation?

3. What do you think could have possibly prompted God to make such a request to one of his choice servants?

Hosea did know this marriage would symbolically mirror God's relationship with Israel, so he realized God had a higher purpose for it. . . . Hosea knew people would look at his family and learn something about the ways of God. To some extent, people today still learn something about God's transforming power through observing what God does in people's lives.
—Gary Smith (*NIV Application Commentary*, 53)

4. Why do you think God chose a marriage metaphor as a symbol of our relationship with him? What do the following verses reveal about marriage and our relationship with Jesus?

Ephesians 5:30–32

John 14:3

Revelation 19:7–9

James 4:4

5. What did Hosea do (1:3)? What does this tell you about his relationship with God?

6. Consider Hosea's and Gomer's daily personal interactions at home. What relational complications can you imagine?

7. Have you ever found yourself betrayed in a dating relationship, engagement, or marriage? Has a family member or friend experienced this? What emotions and challenges accompany these kinds of betrayals?

8. What happened in 1:3 to complicate their relationship even more? Did Hosea have any way of knowing if the child was actually his?

9. Who named the little boy and what was his name (1:4)?

When people saw this little boy, Jezreel, they would be reminded about what had already happened in the Valley of Jezreel in 841 BC. In addition, Hosea would use him as an object lesson concerning a future prophecy. The child's name means "he sows," which will be important later.

What had happened in that valley? Israel's King Jehu had gone too far and slaughtered innocent people to solidify his own political power. God vowed retribution for this unnecessary bloodshed, and that prophecy was fulfilled in 752 BC when Jehu's descendants were assassinated, ending Jehu's dynasty forever.

As Hosea or Gomer walked with their first son through the town hand in hand, the boy reminded the people that if they continued in their adultery toward God, Jehu's fall would be accompanied by their own downfall. In addition, God would "break Israel's bow." This phrase refers to the future destruction of Israel's military might, allowing the powerful aggressor Assyria to make Israel its puppet state and later carry the Jews into exile to serve their captors in a faraway land. This prophecy was fulfilled between 734 and 722 BC.

10. Next, Gomer conceived and gave birth to a daughter (1:6). What did God name her and what did her name mean? In your opinion, what would people think when they saw this little girl or when Hosea used her as an object lesson in one of his sermons?

11. What do verses 6 and 7 tell you about God's emotional responses to Israel's and Judah's adulterous sin?

12. After her daughter was weaned, Gomer gave birth to a third child, a second son (1:8–9). Although the first son may have been sired by Hosea, the next two children were probably not. What did God name this third child and why? What does this name reveal about how God feels about Israel now?

The book of Hosea contains six sermons that reveal God's heart as he pronounces judgment on his disobedient children, followed by sections that show us his redeeming love despite their adulterous sin. We observe the first redemptive oracle in 1:10–2:1. Verse 10 begins with the word "yet," telling us that a contrast follows. These verses read like a love letter.

13. What's the first image God uses to express his unconditional love (1:10)? (See also Genesis 22:17.)

14. Have you ever been unconditionally loved by another person? What impact has this had on your life?

DIGGING DEEPER

Hosea refers to God's covenant with Abraham in 1:10. Is this covenant conditional or unconditional? How does Genesis chapter 15 inform your answer?

15. What's the promise in the second part of verse 10? ("The place" referred to is Israel, and the incident is the birth and naming of Hosea's second son.) What does God call his people now?

A wonderful promise of future restoration immediately follows this gloomy revelation of judgment. It provided encouragement to Hosea's audience by assuring a glorious and secure future for Israel eventually.
—Tom Constable (*Notes on Hosea*, 18)

DIGGING DEEPER

How do these additional prophecies add insight to Hosea's words (Isaiah 9:1–7; 41:8–16; Joel 3:9–21; Amos 9:11–15)?

16. Although God made these initial promises to the Israelites, and he keeps his promises, how might these promises also apply to Christians today? What do the verses below reveal about the family of believers?

Mark 3:20–21, 31, 35

Galatians 6:10

Ephesians 2:19

2 Corinthians 6:18

1 Timothy 5:1–2

17. We all grew up in different family situations—some healthy and some dysfunctional. Some of us may have been orphaned while others enjoyed the company of multiple siblings, cousins, and other relatives. Regardless, when we come to faith in Jesus and accept what he did for us on the cross, we enter into a new family. What does it mean to you that now you are part of God's family "which cannot be measured or counted" (Hosea 1:10)?

DIGGING DEEPER

Will many Jews be part of God's forever family along with Christians? What does Paul say in Romans 11:1–6, 11–16, 25–32?

18. What are ways that you can invest in your new eternal family now?

19. What is Hosea's prophecy in 1:11?

This prophecy has both a near view and a far view, as do many biblical prophecies. The near view occurred after the Jews served out their seventy years in exile and returned to Israel as one united nation where they could openly worship God again. The name Jezreel means "he sows" and may refer to Israel bursting forth in vegetation and plenty as a result. What a great day that was when the Jews returned to the land from captivity. The far view refers to end times when the Jews will reunite in the land under their Davidic king and Messiah, Jesus Christ. What a glorious day that will be!

20. Look back over Hosea 1:1–2:1. What is your overall takeaway? How will this change your heart attitude toward God and your actions right now?

For above all else, the Christian life is a love affair of the heart. It cannot be lived primarily as a set of principles or ethics. It cannot be managed with steps and programs. It cannot be lived exclusively as a moral code leading to righteousness. . . . The truth of the gospel is intended to free us to love God and others with our whole heart. When we ignore this heart aspect of our faith and try to live out our religion solely as correct doctrine or ethics, our passion is crippled, or perverted, and the divorce of our soul from the heart purposes of God toward us is deepened. (Curtis and Eldredge, *Sacred Romance*, 8)

TRUE LOVE IS A SPLENDID HOST

There is love whose measure is that of an umbrella. There is love whose inclusiveness is that of a great marquee. And there is love whose comprehension is of the immeasurable sky. The aim of the New Testament is the conversion of the umbrella into a tent, and the merging of the tent into the glorious canopy of all-enfolding heavens. . . . Push back the walls of family love until they include the neighbour; again push back the walls until they include the stranger; again push back the walls until they comprehend the foe. (Jowett, *Epistles of St. Peter*)

Journeying into the Heart of God

When we desert, neglect, or marginalize our relationship with our heavenly Father, he doesn't desert, neglect, or marginalize us, but he does respond to gain our attention and turn our hearts back to him. He tailor-makes different responses to each of us out of his profound understanding of who we are. After all, he created us, and he knows us better than we know ourselves.

Sometimes he removes "idols" that we love more than him. Sometimes he motivates others to confront us. Sometimes he disrupts our connection with our deception. Sometimes he hedges us in to protect us from temptation. Other times, as a teaching tool, he allows us to experience difficult consequences as a result of our infidelity, but it's never punitive. It's always for our own good.

In my own family, I've seen God remove precious relationships and financial stability, while allowing debilitating sickness to gain the attention of a beloved but wandering Christian. Ultimately that person returned to God, but only after more than twenty years of God's coaxing. And sadly, in 1 Corinthians 11:29–32 we observe rebellious believers experiencing premature death because of their hard hearts, refusal to repent, and destructive witness to the world. I call these severe mercies.

One caution, however: don't assume that if you are experiencing any of these situations that it's because you have been unfaithful to God. We live in a fallen world, and trials occur for multiple reasons. But don't rule out the possibility that your loving heavenly Father seeks your attention. Ask him. He'll show you and help you, always with your best interest at heart.

In Hosea's second sermon, again we'll observe discipline for unfaithfulness and promises of restoration. Hosea writes love poetry to help us truly understand the depth of God's love for us and the magnitude of his pain when we desert, neglect, or marginalize him. Prepare yourself to journey deep into the heart of your God.

OPTIONAL

Memorize
Hebrews 12:5–6
Have you completely forgotten this word of encouragement that addresses you as a father addresses his son? It says, "My son, do not make light of the Lord's discipline, and do not lose heart when he rebukes you, because the Lord disciplines the one he loves, and he chastens everyone he accepts as his son."

THE BACKDROP: BAAL WORSHIP

Since the time of Elijah, many Israelites broke God's heart by worshipping Baal, the pagan Canaanite god of fertility, storm, and rain. Some Jews simply added their Baal worship to their faith in the one true God, but he refused to share his beloved people with a false god. Baal worship involved the cycles of nature needed for prosperity in the ancient world. Baal was the primary god of a pantheon of pagan gods, and he supposedly enabled the earth to produce crops and the people to produce children who would live and thrive. More women died of childbirth than from any other cause. Much of the land was arid, and without water their crops and animals could not survive. As a result, the people depended on the favor of the "gods." When Hosea delivered his sermons, Israel was enjoying a prosperous standard of living. Their markets were full of grain, wine, olive oil, and wool. However, instead of thanking God, many Israelites looked to Baal for their affluence. His sexual-fertility cult temples dotted the countryside where the people practiced ritual prostitution, and some even sacrificed their firstborn to appease Baal and request his favor. Against this backdrop, Hosea's family life illustrated God's response to the adulterous actions and attitude of his beloved Baal-worshipping people.

JUDGMENT ON ADULTEROUS GOMER

At this time in Israel, the penalty for a wife's adultery was death by stoning, and the children of the marriage would usually be orphaned. Within that context, Hosea addresses his children in his poetry. Hosea doesn't carry out either of these "rights," but listen for the fury in God's words as he expresses his righteous anger and exasperation at his beloved's betrayal.

Read Hosea 2:2–7.

1. What does Hosea urge his children to do (2:2)? How does this reflect what's going on in the family?

"You shall have no other gods before me.
   "You shall not make for yourself an image in the form of anything in heaven above or on the earth beneath or in the waters below. You shall not bow down to them or worship them; for I, the LORD your God, am a jealous God."
   —The First and Second Commandments (Exodus 20:3–5)

2. Also in 2:2, Hosea says that Gomer is not his wife nor is he her husband. Most scholars don't believe that this is a statement of divorce. If not, in what sense do you think this statement is true for Hosea and for God regarding their relationship with an unfaithful love?

3. In the second part of verse 2, Hosea, representing God, makes two requests. What are they and what do you think he might mean?

Authentic Christianity is a community of believers so radically committed to Jesus and to each other that it is willing to be countercultural at the point of the world's idolatries and adulteries.
—Howard Snyder (*Flirting with the World*, 13)

4. In the act of stoning an adulterous woman, first the executioners would strip her naked. What do you think was their purpose? If God did this figuratively to his beloved, what do you think might be his purpose?

5. In the latter part of verse 3, Hosea uses desert imagery. In the Bible, what kinds of things happen in the wilderness? Although Israel enjoyed abundant crops and family fertility, in what ways were they living in a "desert"?

Exodus 15:22

Matthew 3:1–2

Luke 4:1–2

Luke 5:16

6. Hosea vents his frustrations in 2:4–5. What makes it difficult for him to show affection to his children?

7. Why has their mother gone after other lovers according to verse 5? (Revisit the note on Baal worship.)

8. In 2:6–7, Hosea considers a strategy to hinder Gomer's actions. What is his plan and what does he hope to accomplish? Put yourself in Gomer's sandals. Do you think this plan would be successful? Why or why not?

JUDGMENT ON ADULTEROUS ISRAEL

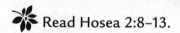 Read Hosea 2:8–13.

Now God speaks through Hosea to philandering Israel who has deserted him to follow Baal. Remember that Gomer figuratively represents Israel as well as all Christians who disappoint or betray God.

9. What had Israel failed to acknowledge and what did she do with those blessings (2:8)?

10. When life goes your way, what is your typical response? Whom do you thank? Do you use those benefits for "Baal," for God, or for yourself?

It won't be long before Israel's prosperity will decline, and the brutal and pagan Assyrian nation will occupy and ultimately kidnap and relocate the Jews to their country to serve as their slaves. Consider how that historical reality fulfills Hosea's prophecies in 2:9–13.

11. How is God going to respond to Israel's infidelity? What does Hosea prophesy in 2:9–13?

2:9

2:10

2:11

2:12

2:13

GOD'S UNCONDITIONAL LOVE

 Read Hosea 2:14–23.

Despite God's deep distress over the unfaithfulness of his beloved, God reveals his true character and devotion even to those who disappoint him.

We see God's long-suffering and loving-kindness and his grace toward us in 2:14–23.

After setting the scene, Hosea writes beautiful redemptive poetry that is broken into three sections, each beginning with "in that day."

Again, this portion of poetry contains both near and far prophecies. Some were fulfilled when the Jewish people returned to Israel after their captivity in Assyria and Babylon. Some are yet to be fulfilled.

12. What is God's strategy to woo his "wife" back in verse 14 and the first part of verse 15? Where does he take her? How does he speak to her?

The Valley of Achor, also known as the Wadi Qelt in the West Bank near Jerusalem, means the "Valley of Trouble," so named because of an event that occurred after Joshua's victory at Jericho (Joshua 7). The Israelites were told not to take any spoils of victory, but Achan disobeyed, and as a result, God allowed them to be defeated at Ai. Ever since, this valley reminded them of this terrible loss and the high price for dishonoring God. When Hosea says that God will make the Valley of Achor into a door of hope, the Jews would know exactly what he meant and would rejoice over God's forgiveness.

13. How does Israel respond in the second part of verse 15? What historical event does Hosea mention that reminded Israel of God's devotion and protection?

THE FIRST "IN THAT DAY"

14. Because of God's amazing grace, what will change in the way God's people relate to him (2:16–17)? (One of the names for Baal was "master.")

15. Who is ultimately responsible for this change? (See Jeremiah 31:31–34.) How will it change our relationship with God?

DIGGING DEEPER

What does Jeremiah 31 reveal about Israel's return from exile both seventy years after their captivity in Assyria and Babylon and in the end times?

THE SECOND "IN THAT DAY"

16. Who will God make a covenant with that will change the way people and nature relate (2:18)? (See also Isaiah 11:6–9.) How will people's lives be impacted?

17. What qualities will characterize God's "marriage" to his beloved in the future (2:19–20)?

18. If you are married, what qualities from 2:19–20 characterize your marriage? What can you do to move your relationship closer to this ideal?

19. If you are single and would like to be married one day, what kind of person do you need to become to make a healthy marriage more likely?

20. If you are called to remain single, how might this picture of an ideal marriage help you create healthy friendships to enrich your life?

THE THIRD "IN THAT DAY"

21. What is the picture described in 2:21–22? What does God say he is going to do? What cycle does that initiate? How do you think the earth will look when God does this?

22. Whom is God speaking about in 2:23? Whose names are mentioned in Hosea's conclusion of the poem that hints at family reconciliation? (See Hosea 1:6, 9.)

23. What have you learned about your One True Love from this lesson? How much does God love you? Have you seen him "fight" for you as he did for Gomer and Israel, and if so, how?

J. I. Packer writes:

> How can jealousy be a virtue in God when it is a vice in humans? God's perfections are a matter for praise—but how can we praise God for being jealous? . . . *There are two sorts of jealousy among humans, and only one of them is a vice.* Vicious jealousy is an expression of the attitude, "I want what you've got, and I hate you because I haven't got it." It is an infantile resentment springing from unmortified covetousness, which expresses itself in envy, malice and meanness of action. It is terribly potent, for it feeds and is fed by pride, the taproot of our fallen nature. There is a mad obsessiveness about jealousy which, if indulged, can tear an otherwise firm character to shreds. . . . But there is another sort of jealousy—zeal to protect a love relationship. (*Knowing God*, 152–54)

This second sort of jealousy is an attribute of Almighty God—a righteous jealousy if his beloved betrays him by running after other lovers. He's zealous for his love relationship with you and grieves when you are not zealous for your love relationship with him.

LOVE PERSISTS WITHOUT RECIPROCATION
BY NATALIE EDWARDS

Jesus loved us before we ever loved him. Before he ever created us, before he ever chose Israel, he knew we would reject him. He knew we wouldn't honor him the way he deserves. He knew we would run to other loves and chase after other pleasures. Yet he still loved us. How? One of the hardest tests of love is continuing to love when the other won't love you back.

Several years ago I met a guy I fell head over heels for, as they say. I really cared about this person and saw goodness in him. I saw honor in him and a gentle yet strong heart that sought to follow the Lord. I got to know him more, and the more I learned about him, the more my feelings grew. I really loved him. But ultimately, he could not reciprocate my love. He'd get close then pull back. Close then pull back. I'd see him often since we lived in the same building, and the stress of it, coupled with the heartbreak, propelled me into a very dark place.

I now have peace knowing it was not meant to be. But at the time it was the greatest pain I've ever walked through. Now, I've had to watch him choose another girl, then get engaged to this other girl . . . and part of me just wanted to let him have it and spill my feelings about how much he hurt me and played games with my heart. But I couldn't. I didn't. God kept reminding me that love doesn't seek its own. It's not selfish. It's not impatient. I knew I needed to be happy for him and let God love him through me the right way.

I kept being his friend. One day I congratulated him. Told him I was happy for him and couldn't wait to see what God does in his life. And I meant it. Then I said goodbye. He moved that day. I haven't seen him since.

As I reflect upon the later portion of that ordeal, somehow it was easy to keep loving him. God did something in my heart. And I discovered what it means to truly care about someone and prioritize their happiness above my own. And what I sensed God telling me over and over again was this: "Natalie, this is how I love you. I love you when you don't choose me. I love you when you don't see value in me. I love you when you find others to comfort you and go everywhere else except to me, the one who loves you the most. Come to me now."

Love will burn you. It will hurt. But I implore you to keep loving. From someone who knows how much it hurts and still believes it's the right way . . . keep loving. Yes, love is a risk. And sometimes, you lose. But the person on the other end of your love needs you to keep loving them, and you need to transform into the kind of person who knows how to love the way Jesus loves. Love persists without reciprocation.

Natalie Edwards is an outstanding intern of mine. Her story is used with permission.

Gangrene and God's Grace | LESSON 3

Gangrene is a medical term describing what can happen if we ignore or fail to treat a wound, burn, or frostbite. Bacteria invade, blood flow with life-giving oxygen is cut off, the area turns red or black, and the body tissue dies. It's gradual and progresses slowly. Sometimes the bacteria cause swelling, hindering disease-fighting antibodies. The bacteria invade and multiply until they produce poisonous toxins and foul-smelling gas, followed by fever, intense pain, and a septic condition that spreads. Without intervention, death is sure.

What gangrene does to the human body, sin does to a person's life and to society. Moral decay is gradual and progresses slowly. People turn away from God. Families become more and more dysfunctional. Disorder and toxicity bring destruction and all kinds of trauma. Without the Great Physician to intervene, depravity and degradation thrive. But praise God! In his mercy, he chose to intervene on behalf of Israel—and in our lives too.

Hosea paints a verbal mural of what occurs when people are left to themselves to contaminate and pollute their own lives and the world around them—and it's not a pretty picture. Ignoring God has rained down various natural consequences since time began. Hosea shows us the kinds of actions and attitudes that break God's heart. As our nation moves further and further away from God, you'll observe similarities with what went on in Israel before God sent them into exile. Don't let this scare you, but let it sober you, and when you see similarities in your life or society, ask how you can be part of the solution. Don't be caught up in playing "ain't it awful"; instead, intentionally shine in dark places.

I'm grateful that Hosea also includes the Great Physician's gracious intervention in his mural. However, as pain often accompanies the physical healing process, it also often accompanies spiritual healing. For many of us, God uses pain and discomfort to break our stubborn pride and make us teachable.

As you work your way through the lesson, remember that although we sometimes neglect our sin until our lives are raw, painful, and gangrenous, God promises gracious healing to all his children in the end.

HOSEA'S MASTERPIECE OF GOD'S GRACE

❉ **Read Hosea 3:1–5.**

Chapter 3 shows us what God's amazing grace looks like, as Hosea fills us in on what's going on now in his family.

1. What does God tell Hosea to do? What has happened to Gomer as a result of her wild living (3:1a)?

2. What does God want Hosea to illustrate to Israel by this action (3:1b)?

3. What do you learn about sacred raisin cakes from Jeremiah 7:18–19 and 44:19? (The "Queen of Heaven" is probably the female pagan deity Ashtoreth, goddess of love and fertility. Hebrew women made these offerings to gain her favor.)

4. What else does 3:2 tell you about what's happened to Gomer?

5. Gomer was a slave to sin and it cost her dearly. What does Romans 6:5–7 say is true for those who belong to God through faith in Christ?

6. However, what can happen to believers who marginalize their relationship with God and neglect to digest his Love Letter (Galatians 4:8–9)?

DIGGING DEEPER

Peter elaborated on these truths in 1 Peter 1:13–23. What additional insights can you glean?

7. Because Hosea "bought" Gomer, in that culture he had the right to expect her to listen to him and cooperate with him. Who has purchased you (Acts 20:28; 1 Corinthians 6:20; 7:23)? How? What difference should this make in the way you respond to God?

8. What does Hosea ask of Gomer in 3:3? What is your heavenly Father asking of you?

In 3:4, Hosea describes what Israel will lack during their seventy years of captivity in Assyria and Babylon. No longer will their own wicked national leaders lead them astray. No longer will they be tempted to practice cultic Baal worship through pagan sacrifices, sacred stones, ephods, household gods, and idols. In this context, the ephod is not the garment worn by the Jewish priest but a cultic object used in Baal worship. Hosea prophesies that God is about to remove the factors that wooed Israel away from him into a place where they will lose the freedom to make their own choices. They will live as slaves to harsh masters and be denied the privilege of worshipping almighty God. They won't enjoy any of the privileges that showed they were God's people, and they will be denied the artifacts they used in idol worship. God's purpose was to soften their hearts and facilitate repentance.

9. In 3:5, Hosea prophesies concerning Israel's return to the land after their exile. This prophecy has both a near and a far meaning. What will happen when Israel returns?

10. King David has been dead for 250 years. What do you think Hosea means when he says they will return and seek their God and David in verse 5? (See Luke 1:29–33.)

DIGGING DEEPER

When David was king, the Lord made a covenant with him, as recorded in 2 Samuel 7. What do you learn about this covenant and how does this amplify Hosea's prophecy in 3:5?

THE EFFECTS OF GANGRENE ON OUR PERSONAL LIVES AND CULTURES

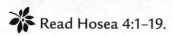 Read Hosea 4:1–19.

Chapters 4–14 record Hosea's sermons. He continues to record his tough-love oracles interspersed with his oracles of grace and encouragement. He delivered these messages to wake up and warn Israel of the impending consequences if they didn't change. Because parts of the sermons are repetitive for emphasis, we won't cover every verse, but we will cover the essence of his messages thoroughly.

Since we will be reflecting on personal, cultural, and societal issues that could bleed over into politics, please refrain from talking about political issues that could lead to dissension.

11. God brings three overarching charges against Israel in 4:1. What are they? Do you think God could make the same charge against people and society today? Why or why not? Can you give a specific example of each charge?

12. Hosea gets specific in 4:2. What does he observe that breaks God's heart? How do these problems affect even those who are not directly committing these sins?

13. What's one consequence of depravity pictured in 4:3? Why is the land drying up? How can both God and people affect nature?

14. Specifically, whom does God accuse in 4:4–9? ("Mother" probably refers to Israel, the motherland.) What is their role in protecting their people from spiritual adultery?

> To the modern Western mind, it might seem unfair that the priests' mothers and children should be punished for their sins. But the concept of corporate guilt and punishment was common in ancient Israel and is frequently reflected in the Hebrew Bible.
> —Robert Chisholm Jr.
> (*Handbook on the Prophets*, 349)

15. Why are the Israelites so vulnerable (4:6)? How is the same problem manifesting itself in society today? How can you be part of the solution?

16. How might religious leaders "feed" off the people and "relish their wickedness" (4:8)?

17. Hosea continues to preach concerning the consequences of worshipping Baal in 4:10–13. Instead of Baal, what "idols" do people "worship" today? What similar consequences do you observe as a result?

18. Although everyone is accountable for their own actions, God takes into account influencing factors when we sin. What does God say about the Israelite women in 4:14? Do you think this principle is still true and if so, what difference does this make for women today?

Verses 15–19 are full of names and places unfamiliar to most of us. I hope these definitions are helpful:

- Judah: This was the name of the Southern Kingdom after the nation split. In verse 15 God warns Israel, the Northern Kingdom, not to influence their fellow Jews in the Southern Kingdom to also be unfaithful to God.
- Gilgal and Beth Aven: These were pagan sites, and God warned the Israelites to stay away from these places, as well as from Mizpah and Tabor (5:1).
- Ephraim: This was one of the most prominent of the ten tribes in the Northern Kingdom and Hosea uses this term to stand for the whole Northern Kingdom.

 Read Hosea 5:1–15.

We observe new insights in several sections of chapter 5.

19. In 5:6, God says that when the Jewish people take animals to the pagan shrines to sacrifice to him, they will not find him there: "he has withdrawn himself from them." What do you think this means (1 Timothy 1:18–20; 1 Corinthians 5:4–5)? Why would a loving God do this to someone he loves dearly?

20. Verses 8–15 predict an upcoming conflict between Israel and Judah because Judah's leaders are "like those who move boundary stones" (5:10). They are cheats who cannot be trusted. As a result, the battle trumpets will sound soon. Whom will Israel turn to for help against Judah? How does that turn out? (5:13)

ADDITIONAL STUDY AIDS

Illegitimate children: This refers to children born as a result of cultic sexual rituals.

New moon feasts: These are pagan celebrations that cause God to continue to burn with jealousy.

Moving boundary stones: This was stealing because it obscured land borders and allowed one person to cheat another.

God is like a moth and rot: These two putrid images picture an insect that devours clothing and the bacteria that eat away at open sores (5:12-13).

People may not always know the extent to which they themselves have syncretized and compromised their beliefs with the philosophies of this world because each of us has an immense ability to be self-deceived (Jeremiah 17:9). Thus, it is important for us to immerse ourselves in the Word of God so that our minds can be transformed by the work of the Holy Spirit. As Hosea indicates, a belief system that simply accepts this world's thinking and combines it with a few Bible verses looks and acts like an unholy prostitution of true faith.
—Gary Smith (*NIV Application Commentary*, 71)

21. Who is actually responsible for the tough love and discipline about to fall on Israel? Hear God's righteous anger in the poetic images as he mourns the state of his relationship with his beloved people and the misery they are bringing on themselves. What is his ultimate purpose in allowing his beloved people to experience this discipline (5:15)? What does this tell you about God and his ferocious love?

22. How do you feel when you observe God disciplining people and nations as consequences for their spiritual adultery? Have you ever been in or seen a situation where you felt tough love was the wisest response? If so, what happened? Why is this kind of love sometimes the best and only alternative?

Understanding and Valuing God's Tough Love

Tough love—the term seems like an oxymoron, words which appear contradictory at first but not when you clearly understand them. I was an adult before I understood the concept of tough love. I grew up in a home where we didn't hug or say "I love you." Love was expressed silently with the purchase of an occasional new toy or pretty dress or by making my favorite dinner or a plate of scrumptious chocolate chip cookies. If I was sick, I was doused with medicine to take away the pain or discomfort. In our family, love meant making you feel better with gifts, food, or the latest fashionable outfit so you could represent the family well. Love made you feel good, at least temporarily.

When I misbehaved, and I often did, the repercussions were harsh, sometimes even spiteful. Demeaning words or some form of humiliation were doled out to control my obstinate resistance. I wasn't loved well, I knew it, and I reacted in defiance. I wasn't an outwardly rebellious teenager, not the pot-sniffing, promiscuous bad girl type, but I was broken, insecure, and seething inside. By my twenties I struggled with clinical depression.

When Jesus rescued me at twenty-four through a women's Bible study, I thought God would show me love the only way I'd experienced it—by giving me tokens of approval that made me feel good—happy relationships, obedient children, a perfect church community, health, fun, and even opportunities to serve him in ways that satisfied my need to feel significant. I was clueless that often it's life's challenges that make us spiritually strong. So when my marriage experienced a rough patch, my children threw tantrums, or my three-year-old daughter needed major surgery, I fought the feeling that God didn't love me. I thought God was hurting me for something I did.

Neither did I understand the concept of discipline for my long-term good. In my stubborn strength, especially in my early years as a believer, I sometimes ignored God's love and direction and acted foolishly. Giving up control and trusting God have been difficult for me because I couldn't trust my parents, and that hindered my trusting God. Just like the Israelites, I've worshipped idols of my own, and God has disciplined me. His purpose

OPTIONAL

Memorize
Titus 2:11–13

For the grace of God has appeared that offers salvation to all people. It teaches us to say "No" to ungodliness and worldly passions, and to live self-controlled, upright and godly lives in this present age, while we wait for the blessed hope—the appearing of the glory of our great God and Savior, Jesus Christ.

wasn't to hurt me but to gain my attention and encourage me to reevaluate my attitudes and actions and return to him.

In situations that would cause me great harm, he used tough love to rescue me from myself and set me on a path that ultimately led to peace and joy, but at the time, those experiences weren't pleasant. I'm grateful that God loves me enough to pursue me with tough love. Don't misunderstand, I'm not saying that every time bad things happen God is sending me to the corner. But sometimes I'm experiencing the discipline of a loving Father, and usually when I ask him, he's been good enough to show me what he's doing and why.

How about you? What do you think when you hear the term *tough love*? Do you think those two words shouldn't go together? Do you understand that God loves you enough to discipline you for your own good when you stray from him? That short-term discipline isn't enjoyable, but it leads to marvelous long-lasting gifts and benefits? Hosea's sermons and prophecies are in our Bible because they show us God's ferocious love and his intense pursuit of his beloved to bring them back to himself. That's Israel. That's Judah. That's Christians today. That's me, and that's you.

Wading through God's expressions of his disappointment and righteous anger with Israel may seem difficult at times. But persevere. Let his words sink deep into your heart. You are listening to the frustrations of the creator God of the universe that still occur when we commit adultery against him—when we turn our backs and shut down our hearts to the God who redeemed us and wants to give us abundant life. Let these realizations act as hindrances to your wanderings and idolatry. Let Hosea's writings about God's tender grace bind you to God and spare you from needing his tough love.

Again, because Hosea sometimes repeats himself, we'll focus on new insights from the texts.

 ## Read Hosea 6:1–3.

In this section, Hosea envisions a conversation between repentant Israelites who determine to leave their adultery and return to God.

1. What do they propose in verse 1?

2. Hosea uses two images of God in verse 1—the image of a lion and the image of a shepherd. These images picture what he's done and what he will do if they repent and return to him as a faithful lover. What has God done? (See also 5:14–15.) What do they believe he will do?

3. What does 6:1 reveal about the character of God?

Bold love is not reckless or cruel. It is not beating up another in the name of sharing or intervention. *Bold love is courageously setting aside our personal agenda to move humbly into the world of others with their well-being in view, willing to risk further pain in our souls, in order to be an aroma of life to some and an aroma of death to others.* —Dan Allender and Tremper Longman III (*Bold Love*, 19)

4. What part do you think God's tough love plays in people's repenting and returning to him? If you have experienced his tough love, how did you respond? What did you learn?

5. In verse 2, Hosea uses a common literary device to approximate time or numbers. Another example is in Proverbs 6:16: "There are six things the LORD hates, seven that are detestable to him. . . ." What do you think Hosea is communicating by using these references to time in verse 2? What's the ultimate result?

6. What do the Israelites and wayward Christians need to do to experience these promises (6:3)?

7. In the latter part of 6:3, Hosea paints several pictures that figuratively reveal what the Israelites can expect after they repent and return to God. What are the pictures and what do you think they represent?

8. Have you experienced light in your darkness or the refreshment of spring rains ending a drought of trials and tribulations in your life after you've repented and sought your First Love? If so, what difference did this make in your life?

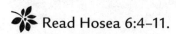

GOD'S RIGHTEOUS JEALOUSY STILL BURNS

Read Hosea 6:4–11.

9. To what does Hosea compare Israel's and Judah's love for God? What do you think he means by using this imagery? Could the Lord say the same about you? (Gilead is a section of Israel east of the Jordan River, and Shechem is a major city.)

10. What does God want from his beloved in 6:6? (See also Matthew 9:10–13.) Since we no longer offer tangible sacrifices in the temple, in what sense would this request apply to us today? To you personally?

Needing a break, I went for a walk in a nearby park. As I headed down the path, a burst of green caught my attention. Out of the mud appeared shoots of life that in a few weeks would be cheerful daffodils, heralding spring and the warmth to come. We had made it through another winter!

As we read through the book of Hosea, it can feel in parts like an unrelenting winter. For the Lord gave this prophet the unenviable task of marrying an unfaithful woman as a picture of the Creator's love for His people Israel (1:2–3). Hosea's wife, Gomer, broke their wedding vows, but Hosea welcomed her back, yearning that she would love him devotedly (3:1–3). So too the Lord desires that we love Him with a strength and commitment that won't evaporate like the morning mist.

—Amy Boucher Pye ("Refreshing Spring Rains")

DIGGING DEEPER

Hosea compares the sins of Israel and Judah to the sins of Adam (6:7). Dissect Genesis 3:1–13 and list similarities.

 Read Hosea 7:1–7.

From 752 to 732 BC, Israel experienced political unrest, intrigue, and sabotage. Several princes assassinated one king after another, only to suffer the same fate themselves, until the nation was leaderless. Hosea compares the hearts of the leaders and the political climate to a hot oven. (Samaria was a town in Israel at that time.)

11. Describe the scene in 7:5–7. What happens? Why? What does this tell you about the state of the nation?

DIGGING DEEPER

To learn more about the political situation in Israel at that time, study 2 Kings 15.

In a foolish attempt to secure her future, instead of going to God with her problems and dealing with internal moral and political failures, Israel made alliances with foreign nations. Douglas Stuart writes, "In 732 BC, Hoshea, after killing Pekah, suddenly shifted from alliance with Egypt, Philistia, and Aram–Damascus to alliance with Assyria. A few years later he broke that alliance, and coming virtually full circle, again sought alliance with Egypt. These confused policies are caricatured in the figurative sense of 'mixed up'" (*Hosea–Jonah*, 121).

Read Hosea 7:8–10.

12. Because Israel mixed herself with other nations, what did she become (7:8)?

13. If you only griddled a pancake on one side, never turning it over, what would that pancake look like eventually? What would hungry people say if you served them a pancake like this? What does this tell you about what Israel had become?

14. Is there any sense in which God might see you as a "flat loaf not turned over"? If so, how will you become beautifully brown and delicious on both sides?

 Read Hosea 7:11–16.

15. Now Hosea compares Israel to a dove. What do you know about doves that might help you understand his meaning?

16. In 7:14–16, we learn more about Israel's actions and attitudes that are breaking God's heart. What new insights can you glean? What consequences will they experience?

THE WHIRLWIND EXILE ANNOUNCED

 Read Hosea 8:1–14.

Trumpets sounded the alarm that a treacherous enemy approached like an eagle about to swoop down and take them away (8:1).

17. In 8:1–6, what reasons are enumerated for the devastating consequences that are about to come upon them?

DIGGING DEEPER

Isaiah explains why worshipping idols is foolish in 44:9–20. What does he argue and how will this help us today even though we tend to worship different kinds of idols?

18. This tornado-like whirlwind will devastate the nation. What specific results are revealed in 8:7–14?

19. God's beloved people had hit bottom. Only God's tough love would shake their shoulders enough to awaken them to their adulterous rebellion. Do you know anyone whom God has allowed to hit bottom in order to awaken them to their sin and bring them back to the loving arms of their God? Has this happened to you? If so, please share discreetly.

20. Why is God's tough love actually a severe form of mercy?

21. What are you learning about the fierce love of God for you and others from Hosea's messages? How can you ensure that God's tough love won't be needed in your life?

RESCUED BY GOD'S TOUGH LOVE

Francis Thompson's father practiced medicine and determined that his son would do the same. Francis gave in to family pressure and attended medical school for nearly eight years but detested his studies, preferring to watch cricket matches and write essays and poetry. After dropping out of school, he fled home and faith, escaping to London to become a writer, without much initial success. He subsisted by working menial jobs, while battling depression and suffering from poor health. Finally, his discouragement led to opium addiction and three homeless years on the streets of London. However, he recovered with the help of a kind woman who gave him a place to stay. In time, he flourished as a writer, and soon after he died, G. K. Chesterton said, "With Francis Thompson we lose the greatest poetic energy since Browning" (*All Things Considered*, 275).

In Thompson's most famous poem entitled "The Hound of Heaven," he described how God had pursued him, despite his defiance and betrayal. Just like with Israel in Hosea, God found ways to get his attention by orchestrating severe mercies and harsh compassions to rescue him. In the poem he wrote of his misguided love of self, of seeking affirmation in other people, lovers, children, and even nature. He wrote of his early life fleeing from God, ignoring him, and going his own way until God finally brought him back through tough love. Here are a few excerpts from the poem.

The Hound of Heaven
by Francis Thompson (1859–1907)

I fled Him, down the nights and down the days;
   I fled Him, down the arches of the years;
I fled Him, down the labyrinthine ways
   Of my own mind; and in the mist of tears
I hid from Him . . .

. . . .

Adown Titanic glooms of chasmèd fears,
   From those strong Feet that followed, followed after.
      But with unhurrying chase,
      And unperturbèd pace,
   Deliberate speed, majestic instancy,
      They beat—and a Voice beat
      More instant than the Feet—
   "All things betray thee, who betrayest Me."

. . . .

(For, though I knew His love Who followèd,
      Yet was I sore adread
Lest having Him, I must have naught beside).

Thompson ended the poem with several stanzas taking on the voice of
God who wooed him back through grace and love:

   "Whom wilt thou find to love ignoble thee,
      Save Me, save only Me?
   All which I took from thee I did but take,
      Not for thy harms,
   But just that thou might'st seek it in My arms.
      All which thy child's mistake,
   Fancies as lost, I have stored for thee at home:
      Rise, clasp My hand, and come!"
         Halts by me that footfall:
         Is my gloom, after all,
   Shade of His hand, outstretched caressingly?
      "Ah, fondest, blindest, weakest,
      I am He Whom thou seekest!"

Experiencing the Abundant Life | LESSON 5

God wired humans with innate desires to live "the good life." What's that? It's our natural desire to want to worship something, to be free from basic want, to belong, to celebrate, to enjoy good health, to contribute, to achieve, to make a difference—in simple terms, to thrive. Through the centuries and in different cultures, the good life has looked different.

In the eighth century before Christ, during Hosea's lifetime, prosperity meant fertility. Thriving meant enough rain and good soil to produce healthy harvests of wheat, barley, olives, grapes, and figs, along with pastures full of healthy sheep, goats, and other livestock for food, transportation, and sacrifices. Fertility included lots of children and large families to work the land and tend the livestock, to pass on the family name, and to care for one another in hard times. Life in Israel centered around producing enough sustenance to live, sacrificing to deities who determined this fertility, and celebrating their favor through festivals.

Crops, flocks, and children were priority one. God told them to trust and follow him and he would provide what they needed. He would bless them with the good life. But pagan Canaanite Baal worshippers all around them insisted that their gods and goddesses were the real source of these gifts. As a result, most Jews decided to worship *both* God and Baal, and in time the demands of Baal lured them away from the true God who cared for them like a devoted husband. They turned their backs on the One who had rescued them from Egypt, fed them in the desert, and given them their promised land of "milk and honey." They prostituted themselves, taking on the role of unfaithful adulterers. They left their authentic source of fruitful abundance for a cheap substitute that didn't have their best interest at heart. Lesson 5 focuses on God's heartbroken response.

Today, the good life looks different. Yet the temptations to abandon God are similar in many ways. In the twenty-first century, people can choose several paths in an attempt to experience the good life.

- They can spend their lives following the voice of secular culture and its promised rewards.

- They can follow a man-made form of "religion" based on working hard to please God and which supposedly results in the good life.
- They can love and follow the Triune God who created them and reveals himself in Scripture and nature, and they can trust him for the peace, joy, and meaning he promises now and for eternity.
- They can choose some combination of the paths above.

As you work your way through Lesson 5, ask yourself, What path or combination of paths have I chosen? In Hosea, God shows himself to be your faithful, loving Husband. Are you his faithful, loving wife? He yearns for your complete devotion. Remember, just like Hosea pursued Gomer, if you choose to stray, God is willing to go to any length to get your attention and woo you back. He loves you that much.

❋ Read Hosea 9:1–17.

Hosea probably delivered this sermon during a feast to celebrate the harvest. Talk about a party pooper! He stood up and admonished the Jews, telling them that their prosperity was about to end because they loved "the wages of a prostitute at every threshing floor" (9:1). Apparently they had added sacred Baal fertility rituals to their Jewish festivals that took place at threshing floors throughout the land. Robert B. Chisholm's notes help us understand what's going on: "At every threshing floor Israel had erroneously attributed the prosperity of her harvests to Baal. She had become an adulteress, offering worship to Baal and receiving from Baal the wages of a prostitute. Those 'wages' were wheat (at the threshing floor), vines and figs, and food, water, wool, linen, oil, and drink. That is, Israel believed that by prostituting herself in worship of Baal that Baal in turn blessed her crops and gave her other necessities of life" ("Hosea," 1398).

1. In verses 1 and 2, Hosea prophesies that God will soon end the Israelites' prosperity. What will God show them about the false god Baal by this action?

2. What do you believe is the source of prosperity in your life? Is there a Baal–like god on the threshing floor of your abundance that you credit with the good life? If so, how do you think you were drawn to this false idol?

3. Not only will their prosperity end in Israel, but what else does Hosea prophesy will soon occur (9:3)? What will they be unable to do there (9:4–5)?

4. What will result from the Israelites' exile into Assyria and Babylon (9:6)? (Note: The Jews were not exiled to Egypt, but Hosea uses this term to mean a place of slavery, since earlier they spent four hundred years in captivity there. Memphis was an Egyptian burial site.)

God declines to sit atop an organizational flowchart. He *is* the organization. He is not interested in being president of the board. He *is* the board. And life doesn't work until everyone else sitting around the table in the boardroom of your heart is fired. He is God, and there are no other applicants for that position. There are no partial gods, no honorary gods, no interim gods, no assistants to the regional gods. God is saying this not because he is insecure but because it's the way of truth in this universe, which is his creation. Only one God owns and operates it. Only one God designed it, and only one God knows how it works. He is the only God who can help us, direct us, satisfy us, save us.
—Kyle Idleman
(*Gods at War*, 23)

5. Who is receiving hateful treatment by the Israelites (9:7)? What do they call him? What has God called him to do and what is life like for him as a result (9:8)?

6. In your opinion, how are Christian leaders treated today? In their ministries? In the secular society? How does God want faithful Christian leaders to be treated? (Hebrews 13:17)

DIGGING DEEPER

To learn more about the incident at Gibeah, read Judges 19–20. What do you learn that enriches your understanding of the culture and God's responses?

In verse 9, Hosea compares the Israelites' sin to corruption in "the days of Gibeah." He refers to the brutal rape and murder of a woman in Judges 19 by a pack of bisexual men. The vile circumstances around this outrage caused the author of Judges to write, "Everyone who saw it was saying to one another, 'Such a thing has never been seen or done, not since the day the Israelites came up out of Egypt. Just imagine!'" (19:30). But Hosea charges the Israelites with the same attitudes and actions as their ancestors during this disgusting time in their history.

7. How does God remember Israel when he first began his relationship with her (Hosea 9:10)?

8. How were their ancestors introduced to Baal worship (Numbers 25:1–3)? What was God's response (Numbers 25:4–5)?

9. Why do you think God responded so harshly to their first worship of false gods at Baal Peor (Hosea 9:10)? How was this a severe mercy? What were the ultimate consequences of these continued temptations and practices for Hosea's audience? What principle can you glean?

DIGGING DEEPER

When the Jews took possession of the promised land, a land flowing with milk and honey, what did God tell them to do (Deuteronomy 7:1–6)? Obviously, they disobeyed this command—the consequences are clear in Hosea. People often criticize God as being harsh because of this and similar commands, but in what sense was God showing his beloved people mercy and kindness? What is the lesson for us?

10. Two attributes of God include his love and his holiness. What happens if we focus on one of these qualities and not the other? What would result in your personal life if you only focused on his love? On his holiness? What do you see in our culture today?

11. Because the Israelites had participated in sacred prostitution as part of Baal fertility rites, what is God going to do (9:11–14)? In what sense do the consequences fit the sins?

12. Because of her sins, Israel would be sent into exile in Assyria for her own good. In addition, what happened to the Jews after they refused to accept Jesus Christ as their Messiah (9:17)? What have they been doing for the last two thousand years?

In AD 70 Rome sacked Jerusalem and the Jewish people scattered throughout many nations, where they've remained for two millennia. Yet they've maintained their identity, heritage, and religious practices without assimilating. Consider this astounding miraculous reality! Only God could facilitate these circumstances as well as return some to their homeland in 1948. God also promises that he will restore them to favor in the last days. In the end, once again they will be his beloved and he will be their faithful Husband. God never gives up! —Sue

✳ Read Hosea 10:1–11:7.

At this time Samaria was a city in Israel. Beth Aven means "house of wickedness" (10:5). No historical record of the battle at Beth Arbel exists (verse 14), but the identity of Shalman may be Shalmaneser V, an Assyrian king who ruled from 727 to 722 BC, or Salamanu, a Moabite king.

DIGGING DEEPER

Study Romans 9–10 for more insight into the Jews' ultimate future.

13. During the exile, what will happen to the calf-idol that the people worshipped as part of their pagan Baal rites (10:5–6)? What message would this send to the Jews as they marched together into exile with the calf-idol accompanying them?

14. What will happen to Israel's leaders and her national status (10:6, 10, 13–15)?

15. What do Isaiah 40:15–17 and 21–24 reveal about God's power related to the rise and fall of nations and their leaders? How might these verses bring you a sense of peace in chaotic times?

16. Hosea paints another family portrait to express his love to Israel and to us, but this time he doesn't use the analogy of a husband and wife. In 11:1–4, how is God like a father? How is Israel like a two-year-old? Have you ever acted this way?

Chastening is not only reconcilable with God's lovingkindness, but it is the effect and expression of it. It would much quieten the minds of God's people if they would remember that His covenant love binds Him to lay on them seasonable correction. Afflictions are necessary for us: "In their affliction they will seek Me early" (Hosea 5:15).
—Arthur Pink (*Attributes of God*, 55-56)

17. In 11:5–7, Israel has become like a rebellious teenager who refuses to listen or heed a loving parent's wise counsel. What does God's tough love look like?

18. Have you ever loved someone with tough love? If you are comfortable, share the situation. How did you feel? What was your hope? Why is tough love sometimes the best or only way to love someone bent on rebellion?

19. What present-day siren-idols threaten your relationship with God? What do they say when they call for your allegiance? Why do you think you are susceptible to this particular idol?

Love is powerful. It drives us to sacrifice ourselves for the sake of another. We want to spend time with the one we love. Eventually, we even start to look like the object of our devotion. God chose the people of Israel and promised to care for them. The Lord loved His people, but they loved false gods and followed all the detestable rituals that those gods required. Eventually, Israel started to look detestable too. As Christians, the way we spend our time, energy, and money shows what we love. If we want to look more like Jesus and grow in our love for Him, we must spend time with Him daily, read His Word, and share our lives with His followers. There's no shortcut to Christlikeness. Have we created margin in our lives to spend the time we need with Christ so that eventually we will look like Him?
—Charles Swindoll (*Swindoll Study Bible*, 1033)

20. As you consider the relationship between God and Israel in this lesson, do you see yourself leaning toward or actually acting on some of the sins that drove a wedge between Israel and God? Specifically, how can you protect yourself from falling into the kinds of traps that severed the fellowship of Israel with the God who loves them so deeply?

FROM THE MIAMI UNDERWORLD TO THE BIG HOUSE FOR JESUS

To Sandi Fatow, like many young women today, the good life consisted of partying, getting high, and hanging out with "cool" people. She just wanted to have fun. Here's her story based on excerpts from the book *Smokin' & Jokin'*:

> I was a hundred-dollar-a day heroin addict back in the '60's. . . . Back then a hundred dollars bought a lot of dope. . . . I never meant to be a junkie. . . . I used to dream about getting married and that I was going to be the bride in the magazines. . . . I dreamed about Mr. Right. . . . Mr. Right was nowhere, but Mr. Wrong was everywhere. (Jacquart 180–81)

Jesse, her first Mr. Wrong, introduced her to her first joint, which led to peyote, cocaine, and LSD. He ended up killing a Florida Highway Patrolman and was electrocuted at Florida State Prison. Next came Freddy, who went to prison for ninety-nine years for murder and armed robbery.

For years, Sandi stayed high and partied in the inner circles of musicians and gangsters, including Jimi Hendrix; Jim Morrison and The Doors; Crosby, Stills, Nash & Young; Tiny Tim; Tommy James and the Shondells; Pete Lucia, known for "Crimson & Clover" and "Crystal Blue Persuasion"; and many others. She got pregnant and gave birth to a baby boy whom she put up for adoption—regrettably, a son she's never seen. Her friends were dying, going to prison, and reaping the fruit of their folly. She had just wanted to have fun. It wasn't supposed to happen that way.

When checking out a Christian rehabilitation facility for a friend, Sandi realized she desperately needed treatment herself. But eighteen hours into withdrawal, she was so sick that she gave up and decided to leave. However, an older woman stopped her, introduced her to Jesus, laid hands on her, and prayed for the strongholds in her life to lose their power. Sandi was instantly delivered from her heroin addiction and set on a new path that night!

She's now married to Steve, who has pastored a church in Knoxville for thirty years. She spends her time speaking for Bill Glass's prison ministries (behindthewalls.com), challenging inmates in prisons all over the world to respond to God's tough love with faith and freedom in Christ.

The Role of Discipline in Forgiveness

OPTIONAL

Memorize
Romans 15:13
May the God of hope fill you with all joy and peace as you trust in him, so that you may overflow with hope by the power of the Holy Spirit.

My children misbehaved from time to time just like everyone else's. I prefer grandparenting because when my grandchildren were small, my job was to make sure they weren't deprived of ice cream, books, and toys. Now that they're older, my duties entail shopping excursions to the mall for school clothes, athletic shoes, and a stop-off at the food court for some delicious, high-calorie junk food.

Certainly we enjoyed fun times when our own children were growing up, but we regarded the task of shaping their character as more important. After all, when you are responsible for guiding them and you love them that much, you want them to be well prepared for adult life. Although we disliked disciplining our children, we worked hard to be consistent and fair. For their own emotional and spiritual health, they needed to change their disrespectful, willful attitudes and actions so they could continue to grow and thrive. Usually, my children responded to discipline with repentance, a softening toward us, and a realization that we had their best interest at heart. And after the tears, I would always hold them, express how much I loved them, and we would talk. I remember these follow-up times as some of the sweetest bonding experiences during those important years.

Whether you have raised children or not, I hope you see the parallels between how we treat those who need our correction and how God disciplines us. In this life, we will never truly blossom until we experience an intimate relationship with the God who created and loves us, followed by a love for others. All this needs to be encased in a dynamic growth process that leads to spiritual and emotional maturity that flows into eternity. This process requires discipline, either our own or God's.

As we continue our journey through Hosea, keep in mind that God deeply desires that we truly mature, and that's the reason God included Hosea's story and sermons in his Love Letter to us. Lesson 6 begins with God's promises that he will bring beloved Israel back from exile. This picture assures us of God's love too (11:8–11). Hosea follows this passage with more insight into why God needed to send Israel into exile in the first place. Look for parallels in your own life.

 **Read Hosea 11:8–11.**

Admah and Zeboyim were cities that God annihilated along with Sodom and Gomorrah for their filth and depravity. For details see Deuteronomy 29:23 and Genesis 19.

Can you recall a sorrowful experience when you were forced to discipline someone you loved for their own good? In Hosea 11:8, God, our beloved Husband and Father, feels overwhelmed with compassion, throws up his hands, and laments that he must discipline Israel so severely. By the way, he feels the same way when he's forced to discipline us.

1. Because God is so grieved, he decides to withhold his total wrath and even makes some promises that will affect Israel's future. What's the promise in 11:9?

2. What is one of the reasons God will show restraint in his discipline (11:9)? How are God's actions different from what we might expect from mankind in a similar situation?

3. Using several images from nature, Hosea pictures Israel's future return from exile in 11:10–11.

Hosea compares God to a mother lion in verse 10. How will God signal his beloved offspring that it's time to come home?

Describe the Israelites' attitude when they return. How have they changed?

In verse 11, Hosea compares the Jews to two different birds. What do you know about these birds that might help us understand what Hosea is trying to communicate?

Why do you think Hosea includes these promises in his sermons?

GOD'S GRIEF OVER DECEIT

 Read Hosea 11:12–12:14.

As much as God hates sending his beloved away, again he lays out reasons why Israel deserves such harsh discipline and why only such drastic means will gain her attention and bring her back.

4. What is God's charge in 11:12? Has anyone ever done this to you? If so, how did you feel? How did it impact your relationship? How do you think God feels if we do this to him?

5. Verse 12:1 lists additional charges.

What do you think Hosea means when he says Israel "feeds on the wind"? (See Ecclesiastes 1:14.)

Do you "feed on the wind"?

What do you think he means when he says they multiply lies and violence?

Why is God wounded when his beloved make alliances with others (Assyria and Egypt) to protect themselves? What are they communicating to God?

In 12:2–6 and 12, Hosea refers to their ancestor and founder of their nation, Jacob. Hosea's audience all knew Jacob's story well. To understand what God wants to communicate to us, we will correlate Hosea's statements about Jacob with related parts of his story in Genesis.

6. Hosea begins by telling us that, like Israel, God saw Jacob's deceit. What happened to Jacob as a result (12:2)?

DIGGING DEEPER

Study Psalm 139:1–18 to learn the depth of God's intimate knowledge of you. Did any parts of the psalm surprise you? What stands out?

7. Do you live knowing that God sees you, cares deeply, and responds emotionally to everything you feel, think, say, and do? If so, how does that affect you? If not, consider spending some time on the Digging Deeper questions in the sidebar.

Does "judgment" scare you? It's vital that you understand the biblical teaching on the two kinds of judgment revealed in Scripture: one for believers and one for nonbelievers.

If you are a believer, Paul tells you in 2 Corinthians 5:9–10: "So we make it our goal to please him [God], whether we are at home in the body or away from it. For we must all appear before the judgment seat of Christ, so that each of us may receive what is due us for the things done while in the body, whether good or bad."

The Greek word for "judgment seat" is *bema*—the place where rewards were handed out during the Olympic Games. We will stand before Jesus at the *bema* seat to give an account of what we do in life, and he will reward us on that basis. We may experience disappointment that we did not live better, but we won't be sent to hell for our failures. Our sins were blotted out by Christ when he paid the penalty for our sins on the cross. And the rewards we receive at the *bema* seat may determine our place of service in Christ's kingdom:

> No longer will there be any curse. The throne of God and of the Lamb will be in the city, and his servants will serve him. They will see his face, and his name will be on their foreheads. There will be no more night. They will not need the light of a lamp or the light of the sun, for the Lord God will give them light. And they [believers] will reign for ever and ever. (Revelation 22:3–5)

These rewards and opportunities to serve are first based on whether or not our names are written in the Lamb's Book of Life (Revelation 20:12). When we trust Jesus alone to forgive our sins by faith alone, our names are written in that book.

The Bible says that nonbelievers will be judged at a different place and time—the "Great White Throne" judgment—because their names are not written in the Book of Life (Revelation 20:15). Their sins will not be covered by Christ, and the holiness of God demands that they pay for their sins themselves.

These realities should cause believers to make their relationship with the Lord top priority. He is our loving Husband, and a natural by-product of our devotion to him will be to please him, abhorring anything that would hinder our intimacy. And living as a thriving, devoted God-lover will show receptive nonbelievers that the true "good life" is lived with him.

Hosea continues to emphasize how much God hates a deceptive heart. As you learn about Jacob, ask yourself if you, in any way, also possess a deceptive heart.

The First Incident

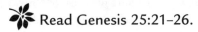 **Read Genesis 25:21–26.**

> Jacob learned how to deceive from his mother. Rebekah mentored him in trickery. To be sure, Jacob had a nature of deception, which we see as far back as his birth. When he came out of the womb, he had hold of the heel of Esau, his older brother. But the heel grabber learned to scheme from his mother. Jacob carries her example the full nine yards. Never underestimate the impact of your character on your children. They are watching to imitate.
> —Charles Swindoll
> (*Swindoll Study Bible*, 50)

8. What happened in the first part of Hosea 12:3 before Jacob was even born that revealed his deceptive heart?

In those days, parents named their children according to their character. Jacob's name means "heel grasper" or "he deceives."

Later Jacob stole his older brother's birthright (Genesis 27), which angered his brother Esau so much that Esau threatened to kill him. The trickery backfired, causing Jacob to flee for his life with no birthright, exiled for many years without family or friends.

Several times in my life, out of good intentions, I've manipulated circumstances to suit my desires, and without exception, I hurt myself and loved ones. I learned the hard way that it's smart to trust God and live his way.

The Second Incident

In the second part of Hosea 12:3 and the first part of 12:4, Hosea refers to a second significant incident in Jacob's life. After many years in exile, he's coming home to attempt reconciliation with his brother Esau—and Jacob is fearful. He asks God for help but also plans a sneaky maneuver by sending a bribe ahead of the meeting, hoping to impress his brother.

❋ Read Genesis 32:22–32 to learn about the turning point in Jacob's life.

9. In verse 24, what happened the night before Jacob met with his brother? (The "man" is actually the angel of God.)

10. What does the angel of God do to Jacob as they are wrestling (32:25)? In your opinion, why?

> Jacob "overcame" or prevailed over the angel—not in the sense of defeating him but in getting the blessing he wanted as he "wept and begged for his favor" (Hosea 12:4).
> —Gary Smith (*NIV Application Commentary*, 173)

11. What happened at daybreak (32:26–28) that illustrates Jacob's desire to change his deceitful heart? How does God bless and reward him?

12. What does Jacob call this place (32:30)? Why?

[Jacob] chose to hold the reins of his life—trying to work out what he felt were God's purposes, in his own way. The results were disastrous! . . . Have you been tempted to run things yourself, to do some scheming? Have you done any spiritual wrestling with God on some issue? . . . Are you searching for answers, for His guidance in a certain matter? Do you question the way He works things out? Perhaps you need to learn more about the eternal plan of God.
      —Luis Palau (*The Schemer and the Dreamer*, 10)

13. What reminder of this incident did Jacob carry with him the rest of his life (32:31–32)? Do you carry any lifelong reminders of poor choices or sin in your life? What do you think is God's purpose in saddling you with these reminders?

14. What do you think Hosea was trying to communicate to the Israelites by comparing them to Jacob when he was wrestling with God? What parallels between Jacob's story and the Israelites' actions in Hosea and their upcoming exile can you discern?

15. Do you have a Jacob in your life? If you are comfortable, share. Consider asking the group to walk with you through this heartbreak in their prayers.

The Third Incident

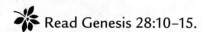 Read Genesis 28:10–15.

16. In Hosea 12:4–6, the prophet mentions another incident in Jacob's life—one that occurred before he wrestled with God. To learn what happened, answer the questions below.

When Jacob was on the run after deceiving his brother, he slept in a place where God communicated to him through a significant dream (Genesis 28:10–15). What did he see in the dream (verse 12)? What is the significance of the fact that the angels were both ascending and descending?

DIGGING DEEPER

For more insight when Jacob returns to Bethel, study Genesis 35:1-15.

The Lord spoke to Jacob during the dream, reiterating the unconditional covenant God had made with Jacob's ancestor Abraham (28:13–15). Why would Jacob need to be reminded of this covenant at this point in his life? Why would Hosea's audience need to be reminded of this covenant right before their exile?

17. Hosea continues to speak of Israel's deceit in Hosea 12:7–8. How were merchants cheating their customers? What convinced these merchants they were still in God's good graces?

18. How important is material wealth to you? Would you make moral compromises to retain it? Does it woo you to devalue growing spiritually? Would you rather be wise than rich?

19. Moses instructed the Israelites to celebrate the Feast of the Tabernacles each year by moving out of their luxurious homes to live in tents for seven days (Leviticus 23:33–44). This exercise would help them appreciate the Lord's blessings and remember the joy of the exodus. What warning does Hosea proclaim if Israel continues in willful rebellion? Why should they know better (12:9–10)?

In 12:11–14, Hosea uses two places, Gilead on the east side of the Jordan River and Gilgal on the west side, to represent the whole nation. The nation is increasing their adultery against God, who reiterates his jealousy and their impending discipline.

 Read Hosea 13:1–3.

20. As Israel falls deeper and deeper into depravity, verse 2 says they "sin more and more." What activity is increasing in Israel that nauseates God (13:2)?

Hosea refers to two patriarchs in 12:12-13. Jacob had to leave his country, family, and friends because of his duplicity and ended up a poor hired hand in the land of Aram where he had to tend animals for many years to pay the bride prices for his wives. Moses, who grew up in Pharaoh's wealthy court, had to flee Egypt as a criminal and also experienced poverty for many years while living in a foreign land. The Israelites would experience this same fate if they did not change their ways.   —Sue

21. As a result of the way Israel worshipped and lived, God, their beloved Husband, warned them that he would exercise tough love and send them away. They would soon disappear from his sight and from the home they loved. To convey this message, Hosea used four pictures in 13:3. What are they?

22. God grieves deeply when he's forced to exercise tough love. Can you relate? Has anyone in your life disappeared this way? If so, how did you feel when this occurred? How do you feel now? What are your hopes and prayers for them? Have they returned better off for the experience?

23. Has your study of God's tough love in Hosea helped you find peace in your own situation? Why or why not?

WHEN TOUGH LOVE HURTS THE MOST

I found trusting God for myself easier than trusting God for my children. Once, out of a fierce desire to protect my child, I brought God's tough love down on us both. Here's how it happened.

My youngest daughter attended a large secular university where campus housing was at a premium. Her second year, she was accepted into one of the nicest dorms on campus, but the rule was that you could either choose the room *or* the roommate of your choice but not both. I had heard horror stories of what happened when you roomed with some girls—like men in the room all night—and I turned into mother bear. I was not going to allow my child to take potluck in roommates, nor were we willing to give up that choice room.

I had heard that if your child had a learning disability they would ditch the rule. So I decided to make my case with the administrator who could fix this "unfair" situation. All week, I was on the phone long distance, climbing my way up the ladder to the gentleman who could give my daughter the room *and* the roommate she deserved.

Finally, I was on the phone with him. We talked for a few minutes, and then he asked me, "Does your daughter have a learning disability?" I answered rather indignantly, "Well, I prefer not to label people." That did it. He bought it. I had done the impossible. I called my daughter, she turned cartwheels on the other end of the phone, and we rejoiced together.

Only the roommate she had chosen, the dear Christian girl from her church, did not turn out to be the roommate we expected. In fact, she *did* have men in the room all night, a lot. And she went home at Christmas under suspicious circumstances. All fall I had to endure calls from my daughter, who was trying to figure out how to navigate this awkward situation. And it was my fault, so not only was I suffering for my deception, but what hurt the most was that my beloved daughter had to pay the consequences too.

God sometimes needs to use tough love in the form of a two-by-four to get our attention and break us of our control issues and lack of faith. This was one of those times for me and for my daughter. Now, when we are tempted to go our own way rather than trusting God, we look at each other, remember, smile, and determine to make a wiser choice.

God knows what he is doing in our lives. So trust him, follow him. Two-by-fours hurt. You won't regret trusting your sovereign Father who has all our best interests at heart—even when he must resort to tough love.

"Happy Endings" | LESSON 7

Are you tired of learning about God's tough love? It's a heavy topic that requires us to think deeply, which can be exhausting. But imagine how sick and tired God must be as he beholds the constant depravity of his creation! Even more, how he must grieve over the betrayals and ingratitude of his beloved over the centuries. The Holy One has every right to punish us for our sins for eternity—but that's not who he is. His ferocious love demands otherwise!

As Hosea concludes his sermons, we see that God's tough love has done its work. God has the Israelites' attention. They've repented and softened their hearts; they've learned their lesson. Finally, Hosea and Gomer are reunited, sins forgiven, and their children returned to a healthy family. Don't you just love happy endings?

Hosea's life has been one huge metaphor for God's work in the world. Mercy, grace, and justice win. But wait, how can justice win when there's been no complete reckoning for sin? The Jews will still sin after they return home, and so do we—even though our love relationship with God has been restored. What's missing to make our happy ending possible? Jesus! God's permanent forgiveness of sin requires a once-for-all reckoning. Justice demands it. And there is.

What Hosea and the Israelites didn't know is that God would send his only Son Jesus to pay the penalty for all sins so that everyone who believes in him may join God's family, washed clean. That sacrifice would be retroactive and cover the sins of faithful Jews too. Through Christ, this cleansing opens the door into a beautiful, new, and even more intimate relationship with God for all who desire to come. Home is restored. And, as we've seen, the Bible reveals that in the end, faithful Jews will come back home too.

As we conclude our trek through Hosea's love life and sermons, persevere through just a little more tough love and then sing hallelujah as Hosea reveals God's ferocious love. It's shining brilliantly like a diamond against a black velvet background. Celebrate with Hosea as he heralds God's promises of restoration, grace, joy, and blessings. You've weathered

OPTIONAL

Memorize
Romans 8:1–2
Therefore, there is now no condemnation for those who are in Christ Jesus, because through Christ Jesus the law of the Spirit who gives life has set you free from the law of sin and death.

Therefore, if anyone is in Christ, the new creation has come: The old has gone, the new is here! All this is from God, who reconciled us to himself through Christ and gave us the ministry of reconciliation: that God was reconciling the world to himself in Christ, not counting people's sins against them. And he has committed to us the message of reconciliation. We are therefore Christ's ambassadors, as though God were making his appeal through us. We implore you on Christ's behalf: Be reconciled to God.
—2 Corinthians 5:17–20

the darkness, but only that journey can enhance the brightness of the light now revealed. God's ferocious love for you and me is real! A thousand hallelujahs! Savor them all, and then, out of gratitude, with your affection and lifestyle, delight rather than disappoint him.

A SEVENTY-YEAR DISCIPLINE DECLARED

 Read Hosea 13:4–16.

This is what the LORD says: "When seventy years are completed for Babylon, I will come to you and fulfill my good promise to bring you back to this place. For I know the plans I have for you," declares the LORD, "plans to prosper you and not to harm you, plans to give you hope and a future. Then you will call on me and come and pray to me, and I will listen to you. You will seek me and find me when you seek me with all your heart."
—Jeremiah 29:10–13

1. In 13:4–6, Hosea recounts God's care for Israel through her history, first in the exodus out of Egypt, then in the wilderness when he fed her manna and quail, and finally in his blessings in the promised land of "milk and honey." What does God expect of Israel as a result (13:4)? What does he expect of us?

2. What can easily occur when we are enjoying God's bounty and blessings (13:6)?

3. Do you tend to draw closer to the Lord when life goes well or when challenges occur? Can you discern why? How might you rectify this tendency?

A nation of farmers and shepherds, Israel depended on livestock for survival. They worked hard to protect their flocks from vicious wild animals native to that region—lions, leopards, and bears. Particularly dangerous were the females protecting their cubs. Through imagery Israel would graphically understand, God announced impending discipline with a horrifying picture (13:7–8). God had given them every opportunity to repent, but his patience was over. Soon they would be in the hands of brutal nations who act like wild beasts—Babylon and Assyria.

> This is the bitterest of all—to know that suffering need not have been; that it has resulted from indiscretion and inconsistency; that it is the harvest of one's own sowing; that the vulture which feeds on the vitals is a nestling of one's own rearing. Ah me! This is pain!
> F. B. Meyer (*Christ in Isaiah*, 10)

4. Why does God feel justified to take this drastic action (13:9)?

5. Who will be unable to help Israel as she is carried off into captivity for seventy years (13:10–11)?

6. Do you look to political leaders to bless you? Why is this ultimately futile? Nevertheless, what's our responsibility to our governing leaders (Romans 13:1–7)?

7. In 13:12–13, Hosea compares Israel and those who foolishly rebel against God to senseless children. After its mother's long, excruciating labor, what does this senseless child refuse to do? What pain does this cause the mother? What will Israel miss as a result of her stubbornness?

8. The hot east wind that's about to blow in from the desert is the pagan power Assyria. Who has sent her? What will she do to Israel (13:15–16)?

DIGGING DEEPER

What will ultimately happen to Babylon for her harsh treatment of the Jews (Jeremiah 25:11–14)?

9. How does God feel about being forced to exercise tough love (Jeremiah 8:21–9:1)?

This passage [Hosea 13:4–16] is about God's past grace to Israel and the death of the nation Israel, not any nation today. It is inappropriate to apply these predictions of national disaster and war to any group of people today. The value in such a passage is that it provides key insights into the way God works with people.
—Gary Smith (*NIV Application Commentary*, 189)

DISCIPLINE ACCOMPLISHED, BLESSINGS RESTORED

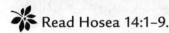 Read Hosea 14:1–9.

Israel fell in 722–721 BC. A remnant began their pilgrimage home seventy years later.

10. Just as Hosea invited Gomer back into their marriage, God invites Israel back into an intimate love relationship with him. What must she do first (14:2)? What additional insight does John give us in 1 John 1:9–10?

Day after day every priest stands and performs his religious duties; again and again he offers the same sacrifices, which can never take away sins. But when this priest [Jesus] had offered for all time one sacrifice for sins, he sat down at the right hand of God.
—Hebrews 10:11–12

11. The Bible says our sins are forgiven—past, present, and future—yet God asks us to practice the discipline of self-examination and repentance. Why do you think God asks us to do this?

12. Do you keep a clean slate before God by confessing your sins regularly? Why or why not?

13. What attitude alterations does God request (14:3)? Why? What has Israel learned?

14. What does God promise in 14:4–8? God made these promises reality in several ways. What do the passages below reveal?

Isaiah 53:4–6

Jeremiah 23:5–6

Jeremiah 31:31–34

Dissect all of Isaiah
53 for beautiful truths
about Jesus, who he is
and what he's done.

Jeremiah 32:37–41

15. How has God invested in our relationship with him as church-age believers that Hosea's audience did not experience or know about? What's our reasonable response (Romans 12:1–2)?

FRUITFULNESS RESTORED

16. Hosea uses pictures from nature as a contrast to his sermons full of deserts and desolation (14:5–7). What do these images teach us about the fruitfulness that God provides his beloved?

The morning dew

The beautiful lily

The giant cedar of Lebanon

The olive tree

Fields of grain

Plentiful vineyards ripe with grapes

17. Blessings from God don't ensure we'll be healthy and wealthy. In this fallen world, challenges still fall on us all. But what does God promise those who make their love relationship with him top priority and live faithfully in that beautiful union (Romans 8:37–39)?

Therefore we do not lose heart. Though outwardly we are wasting away, yet inwardly we are being renewed day by day. For our light and momentary troubles are achieving for us an eternal glory that far outweighs them all. So we fix our eyes not on what is seen, but on what is unseen, since what is seen is temporary, but what is unseen is eternal.
—2 Corinthians 4:16–18

18. What serious dangers must Israel guard against (14:8)? During the course of our study together, what have you learned about which of these serious dangers are most problematic for you? How will you protect yourself in the future?

19. In the second part of 14:8, God describes himself as a flourishing juniper. This is an evergreen plant in Israel that can take several forms, from a desert shrub that furnishes shade for weary travelers and fuel for their fires to a tall, fragrant pine tree. What is God saying to us when he uses this imagery to describe himself?

In verse 9, Hosea asks us a final question: "Who is wise?" He's probably asking each of us, "Are you wise?" Wisdom is more than knowledge. It's living in a right relationship with God that results in the good life, as defined by God.

20. How has your study in Hosea made you wiser? What insights have you gleaned to help you, unlike Gomer, be a faithful wife living out a beautiful union with your One True Love that results in joy, peace, fruitful service, and the good life now and for eternity?

This is Hosea's open secret: God is the Lover of Israel. God loves his people with a sacred love. He won't let go. Israel's love is to be sacred. So, when the *Jesus Creed* [Matthew 22:37–40] calls us to love God with all our heart, soul, mind, and strength, we are called to form a love relationship with God that is utterly sacred.

—Scot McKnight
(*Jesus Creed*, 45)

21. What have you learned about the character of God, his emotions, his heart, his love for you? How will this understanding influence your love relationship with him from now on?

It was only when I lay there on rotting prison straw that I sensed within myself the first stirrings of good. Gradually it was disclosed to me that the line separating good and evil passes not through states, nor between classes, nor between political parties either—but right through every human heart—and through all human hearts. . . . And that is why I turn back to the years of my imprisonment and say, sometimes to the astonishment of those about me: *"Bless you, prison!"*
—Aleksandr Solzhenitsyn (*Gulag Archipelago*, 312–13)

May the God of hope fill you with all joy and peace as you trust in him, so that you may overflow with hope by the power of the Holy Spirit.
—Romans 15:13

For many of my early Christian years, I struggled to believe God really loved me. I knew myself too well. I battled an overly sensitive nature, a tendency toward extreme highs and lows, a drive to think first of my own personal benefit (selfishness), a desire to control my environment and the people around me, irrational fears, too much focus on comfort, and . . . I could go on but enough—you get the idea. A strong-willed, passionate nature has led to positives in my life, but it's also gotten me into tons of trouble, especially before God enabled me to curb and counter these tendencies.

I've earned my share of hard knocks, all duly deserved from the hand of a caring Father. Yet as we've walked together through the years, like the weaker oxen in the shared yoke, I've come to understand that God's love isn't dependent on me, but I'm loved because that's who God is. My heart is his and he loves me the way good parents love their children regardless of whether they are courageously taking their first steps or pouting in the corner.

As I've kept his Word close, delving into books like Hosea, his strong arms have held and directed me into a rich, blessed life of joy and peace. I suppose I'll not be completely free of his tough love until I pass into his glorious light, but I'm glad that he never left me alone to flounder on my own but loved me enough to correct and guide me. Tough love is real love, and I'm grateful. Don't fight it. Learn from it, and enjoy the incredible benefits of a teachable spirit. May his tough love bless you too.

Works Cited

Allender, Dan B., and Tremper Longman III. *Bold Love*. Colorado Springs: NavPress, 1992.

Bramer, Stephen J. "Suffering in the Writing Prophets (Isaiah to Malachi)." In *Why, O God? Suffering and Disability in the Bible and the Church*, edited by Larry J. Waters and Roy B. Zuck, 147–60. Wheaton, IL: Crossway, 2011.

Chesterton, G. K. *All Things Considered*. London: Methuen, 1908.

Chisholm, Robert B., Jr. *Handbook on the Prophets*. Grand Rapids: Baker Academic, 2002.

———. "Hosea." In *The Bible Knowledge Commentary: Old Testament*, edited by John F. Walvoord and Roy B. Zuck. Wheaton, IL: Victor, 1985.

Constable, Thomas L. *Notes on Hosea*. Sonic Light. 2017 edition. http://planobiblechapel.org/tcon/notes/pdf/hosea.pdf.

Curtis, Brent, and John Eldredge. *The Sacred Romance: Drawing Closer to the Heart of God*. Nashville: Thomas Nelson, 1997.

Elliot, Elisabeth. *Quest for Love: True Stories of Passion and Purity*. Grand Rapids: Revell, 2002.

Feinberg, Charles Lee. *Hosea: God's Love for Israel*. The Major Messages of the Minor Prophets 1. New York: American Board of Missions to the Jews, 1947.

Ford, Cristina. "Why Does Mom Prefer Hallmark Movies at Home over Going to the Theater?" Crosswalk.com. November 28, 2017. https://www.crosswalk.com/blogs/christian-trends/why-are-hallmark-movies-so-popular.html.

Holmberg, Kirsten. "Direct Instructions." *Our Daily Bread®*. March 9, 2018. Copyright © 2018 by Our Daily Bread Ministries, Grand Rapids, MI. Reprinted by permission. All rights reserved.

Idleman, Kyle. *Gods at War: Defeating the Idols That Battle for Your Heart*. Grand Rapids: Zondervan, 2013.

Ironside, Harry A. *Notes on the Minor Prophets*. New York: Loizeaux Brothers, 1947.

Jacquart, Joanne. *Smokin' & Jokin': The Sandi Fatow Story.* Dallas: Acclaimed, 2016.

Jensen, Irving L. *Minor Prophets of Israel: A Self-Study Guide.* Chicago: Moody Press, 1975.

Jowett, John Henry. *The Epistles of St. Peter.* oChristian.com. Accessed July 25, 2018. http://articles.ochristian.com/article18767.shtml.

Kent, Carol. *Secret Longings of the Heart: Overcoming Deep Disappointments and Unfulfilled Expectations.* Colorado Springs: NavPress, 1990.

Long, Stephanie Topacio. "11 Romance Readers Reveal Why They Love the Genre." *Bustle.* September 8, 2016. https://www.bustle.com /articles/181652-11-romance-readers-reveal-why-they-love-the -genre. (Warning: this website contains some inappropriate content that neither Kregel Publications nor I endorse.)

McCracken, Brett. "Formulaic for a Reason: The Existential Appeal of Hallmark Movies." *The Gospel Coalition.* November 28, 2017. https://www.thegospelcoalition.org/article/formulaic-reason -existential-appeal-hallmark-movies/.

McGee, J. Vernon. *Thru the Bible with J. Vernon McGee: Proverbs–Malachi.* Vol. 3. Nashville: Thomas Nelson, 1983.

McKnight, Scot. *The Jesus Creed: Loving God, Loving Others.* Brewster, MA: Paraclete Press, 2005.

Meyer, F. B. *Christ in Isaiah.* New York: Fleming H. Revell, 1895.

Packer, J. I. *Knowing God.* Downers Grove, IL: InterVarsity, 1993.

Palau, Luis. *The Schemer and the Dreamer: God's Way to the Top.* Portland, OR: Multnomah Press, 1976.

Pink, Arthur W. *The Attributes of God.* Grand Rapids: Baker, 1975.

Pye, Amy Boucher. "Refreshing Spring Rains." *Our Daily Bread®.* March 21, 2017. Copyright © 2017 by Our Daily Bread Ministries, Grand Rapids, MI. Reprinted by permission. All rights reserved.

Smith, Gary V. *The NIV Application Commentary: Hosea, Amos, Micah.* Grand Rapids: Zondervan, 2001.

Snyder, Howard A. Foreword to *Flirting with the World: A Challenge to Loyalty,* by John White. Wheaton, IL: Harold Shaw, 1982.

Solzhenitsyn, Aleksandr. *The Gulag Archipelago Abridged: An Experiment in Literary Investigation.* New York: HarperCollins, 2007.

Stuart, Douglas. *Hosea–Jonah.* Word Biblical Commentary 31. Waco, TX: Word, 1987.

Swindoll, Charles R. *The Swindoll Study Bible.* Carol Stream, IL: Tyndale House Publishers, 2017.

Thompson, Francis. "The Hound of Heaven." In *Poems.* London: Burns and Oates, 1893.

Verrillo, Erica. "What Are the Most Popular Literary Genres?" *Medium.* The Writing Cooperative. November 15, 2017. https://writingcooperative .com/what-are-the-most-popular-literary-genres-6db5c69928cc.

Wood, Leon J. "Hosea." In *The Expositor's Bible Commentary, Volume 7: Daniel and the Minor Prophets*, edited by Frank E. Gaebelein, 161–228. Grand Rapids: Zondervan, 1985.

Yancey, Philip. *What's So Amazing About Grace?* Grand Rapids: Zondervan, 1997.

About the Author

Sue Edwards is professor of educational ministries and leadership (her specialization is women's studies) at Dallas Theological Seminary, where she has the opportunity to equip men and women for future ministry. She brings over forty years of experience into the classroom as a Bible teacher, curriculum writer, and overseer of several megachurch women's ministries. As minister to women at Irving Bible Church and director of women's ministry at Prestonwood Baptist Church in Dallas, she has worked with women from all walks of life, ages, and stages. Her passion is to see modern and postmodern women connect, learn from one another, and bond around God's Word. Her Bible studies have ushered thousands of women all over the country and overseas into deeper Scripture study and community experiences.

With Kelley Mathews, Sue has coauthored *New Doors in Ministry to Women: A Fresh Model for Transforming Your Church, Campus, or Mission Field* (second edition releasing 2020); *Women's Retreats: A Creative Planning Guide*; and *Leading Women Who Wound: Strategies for an Effective Ministry*. Sue and Kelley joined with Henry Rogers to coauthor *Mixed Ministry: Working Together as Brothers and Sisters in an Oversexed Society*. *Organic Mentoring: A Mentor's Guide to Relationships with Next Generation Women*, coauthored with Barbara Neumann, explores the new values, preferences, and problems of the next generation and shows mentors how to avoid potential land mines and how to mentor successfully. Her newest book, *Invitation to Educational Ministry: Foundations of Transformative Christian Education*, coedited with George M. Hillman Jr., DTS vice president of student life and professor of educational ministries and leadership, serves as a primary academic textbook for schools all over the country as well as a handbook for church leaders.

Sue has a doctor of ministry degree from Gordon-Conwell Theological Seminary in Boston and a master's in Bible from Dallas Theological Seminary. With Dr. Joye Baker, she oversees the Dallas Theological Seminary doctor of ministry degree in Christian education with a women-in-ministry emphasis.

Sue has been married to David over forty-five years. They have two married daughters, Heather and Rachel, and five grandchildren. David is a retired CAD applications engineer, a lay prison chaplain and founder of their church's prison ministry, and a former DTS student. Sue loves fine chocolates and exotic coffees, romping with her grandchildren, aquacise, and taking walks with David and her two West Highland Terriers, Quigley and Emma Jane. David and Sue now attend Northwest Bible Church in Dallas.

The Discover Together Bible Study Series

Inductive Bible studies for women from Sue Edwards, including:

Daniel: Discovering the Courage to Stand for Your Faith
Philippians: Discovering Joy Through Relationship
Ecclesiastes: Discovering Meaning in a Meaningless World
Galatians: Discovering Freedom in Christ Through Daily Practice

And many more!

Learn more at DiscoverTogetherSeries.com

Kregel
Publications

Forget outdated ideas— become the perfect mentor for the next generation!

Organic
MENTORING

A MENTOR'S
GUIDE TO
RELATIONSHIPS
WITH NEXT
GENERATION
WOMEN

SUE EDWARDS & BARBARA NEUMANN

"If you're an older woman who has longed to impart the wisdom you've gleaned from the years but weren't sure how to go about it, get this book!"
—**Halee Gray Scott**, PhD, author of *Dare Mighty Things*

"Young women are desperate for mentors to guide them in thriving mentoring relationships that help heal their brokenness. *Organic Mentoring* sheds light on why traditional methods flounder and offers fresh, insightful, and useful suggestions to meet the challenges of mentoring next generation women."
—**Elisa Morgan**, speaker, author

Kregel
Publications